BUBBLY, SCRUBBY HANDS

COUNTING, ADDING, PLAYING, CLAPPING,
THAT'S WHAT HANDS ARE FOR!

STICKY, DIRTY, SWEATY, GERMY
ON YOUR HANDS AND MORE!

UN-GRUB THEM, SCRUB THEM, RINSE AND RUB THEM,
LIKE A HAND WASHING MACHINE!

HI-FIVES, HANDSHAKES, THUMB WARS, FIST BUMPS,
ARE BETTER WHEN YOUR HANDS ARE CLEAN!

ALWAYS WASH YOUR
HANDS BEFORE
MAKING MEALS.

1

Protein helps us to grow and make muscles. Protein is found in meat, chicken and fish. It is also in nuts and some beans. Milk, eggs and cheese are also good sources of protein. But remember, protein can have a lot of fat that is not so good for us, so choose the low fat kinds of these foods.

Vitamins are found in a lot of foods we eat everyday. There are many types of vitamins. Our bodies need them to grow and stay healthy. Fruits and veggies, milk and eggs, nuts and meat all contain one or more vitamin. Vitamins are named for letters in the alphabet: A, B, C, D, E and K. Examples are: Vitamin A, found in carrots and sweet potatoes, helps you see well, even in the dark. Vitamin C, found in blueberries and strawberries, helps you heal if you scrape your knee. Vitamin D, found in milk and eggs, helps to build strong bones.

Oil is all fat, so you only need a little. Cooking foods in only oil will give you too much fat. Try cooking with chicken broth instead of oil. Another healthy way to cook is to grill or bake.

Sugar is sweet and it tastes good. But it is one of those carbs that get used up fast, which means it only gives you a short burst of energy. Too much sugar can make us gain weight and give us cavities in our teeth. Soda and candy have a lot of sugar in them so these should be sometime treats, not everyday things.

2

eat...so eat well!

Calcium is a mineral that helps to build bones and teeth. Growing kids need calcium almost every day. Milk, yogurt and cheese are good sources. Choose the low fat versions of these foods.

Carbs - short for carbohydrates (car·bo·hy·drate) – give us the fuel our bodies need to stay active. There are different types of carbs. Some get used up fast like sugar or white bread. Others last longer like beans or whole wheat bread. Try choosing the carbs that last longer so your energy lasts longer!

Fat: Our bodies need some fat, but only a little to stay healthy. Fats are found in a lot of foods. Some of these foods include butter, oil, meat and ice cream. Fat can also be added by the way we cook food, such as frying foods - think of French fries and potato chips. Too much fat can make us gain weight and be bad for our hearts. To avoid too much fat in your diet you should eat less fried foods, candy and cookies. Choose low fat milk and cheese, and take the skin off chicken. Also, instead of fried or breaded chicken, try grilled or baked.

Fiber helps to keep you full longer. It is found in fruits, veggies, beans, brown rice and whole wheat bread.

3

Banana-sicle & Yogurt

ALEXIA A. AGE 10, OHIO

Nutrition:
Servings: 1
Calories: 209
Calories from Fat: 17
Total Fat: 1.8g
Saturated Fat: 0.9g
Cholesterol: 3mg
Sodium: 64mg
Carbohydrates: 43.1g
Dietary Fiber: 3.3g
Protein: 5g

Ingredients:
1 Banana
1/8 cup Low Fat Granola
¼ cup Low Fat Vanilla Yogurt
Popsicle stick

Instructions:
Put banana on a popsicle stick.
Dip banana in yogurt (covering banana).
Roll banana covered in yogurt in granola.
Freeze for one hour.

THIS TREAT IS GOOD FOR YOU AND FUN TO MAKE!

KIT SPROCKETTE

This is a great snack if you are going to be active after school. It is also a healthy snack low in fat that contains protein and calcium for growing bodies, carbohydrates for energy and fiber to fill you up till dinner.

4

Bitty Cracker Tomato Soup

HANNAH S. AGE 10, OHIO

DARBY BOINGG

Ingredients:
8 oz. Tomato Soup, condensed
4 oz. 1% Low Fat Milk (about ½ cup)
2 oz. Cheese Crackers
1 oz. Shredded Cheddar Cheese (about ½ cup)

Instructions:
Prepare soup with milk.
Top with crackers and cheese.

Nutrition:
Servings: 4
Calories: 153
Calories from Fat: 64
Total Fat: 7.1g
Saturated Fat: 3.3g
Cholesterol: 10mg
Sodium: 513mg
Carbohydrates: 17.2g
Dietary Fiber: 0.6g
Protein: 5g

Apple Cinnamon Wrap Up

JOSEPHINE R. AGE 10, OHIO

AN APPLE A DAY...

CONSTANCE
EATRITE

Ingredients:
1 tsp. Ground Cinnamon
2 tsp. Butter (salted), whipped
1 Soft Flour Tortilla
3 oz. Apples with Skin, sliced (about ½ cup)

Instructions:
Spread butter on tortilla.
Add apple slices onto tortilla.
Sprinkle cinnamon onto apples.
Roll up tortilla.
Microwave for 1 minute.

Nutrition:
Servings: 1
Calories: 292
Calories from Fat: 86
Total Fat: 9.5g
Saturated Fat: 4.2g
Cholesterol: 14mg
Sodium: 324mg
Carbohydrates: 46.3g
Dietary Fiber: 5.4g
Protein: 5.3g

6

This can be a healthy snack if you use whole wheat tortillas
or sandwich wraps. Also be sure to go easy on the butter.
The wrap and apples provide the fiber.

Peanut "Butter-Fly" Toast & Apples

MACKENZIE S. AGE 10, OHIO

Ingredients:
1 Slice Whole Wheat Bread
1 Tbs. Smooth Peanut Butter
3 oz. Apples with Skin, sliced (about ½ cup)

THIS IS AN AWESOME SNACK OR BREAKFAST ON THE GO!

SPIKE ARMSTRONG

Instructions:
Toast bread.
Spread peanut butter onto bread.
Top with apple slices.

Nutrition:
Servings: 1
Calories: 236
Calories from Fat: 88
Total Fat: 9.8g
Saturated Fat: 2g
Cholesterol: 0mg
Sodium: 233mg
Carbohydrates: 29.9g
Dietary Fiber: 5.4g
Protein: 7.2g

This is a healthy snack because it gives you protein, carbohydrates and fiber. Just make sure to use whole wheat bread and not too much peanut butter.
Peanut butter is good for you, but it's high in calories, which is why you have to watch how much you eat.

Eggs in a Basket

DAKOTA S. AGE 11, OHIO

THIS RECIPE IS SUNNY SIDE UP!

KIT SPROCKETTE

Ingredients:
1 Large Egg
1 Slice Whole Wheat Bread

Instructions:
Cut a hole in the center of the bread.
Place bread in a skillet .
Crack the egg into the hole of
the bread.
Let egg cook.

Nutrition:
Servings: 1
Calories: 154
Calories from Fat: 71
Total Fat: 8g
Saturated Fat: 2.1g
Cholesterol: 211mg
Sodium: 294mg
Carbohydrates: 12.1g
Dietary Fiber: 1.7g
Protein: 8.6g

This simple meal provides protein and carbohydrates.
Be sure to use whole wheat bread and non-stick cooking
spray instead of butter as a healthy alternative.

Happy Sandwich Delight

LAYLA G. AGE 10, OHIO

A HEALTHY SANDWICH MAKES A HAPPY BELLY!

Ingredients:
Two Slices Whole Wheat Bread
¼ cup Lettuce
1 Tomato Slice
4 oz. Oven Roasted White Turkey Breast
1 Tbs. Mayonnaise
1 Tbs. Mustard

Instructions:
Put mayonnaise on one piece of bread and mustard on the other piece.
Add tomato, lettuce and turkey to one piece of bread and cover with other piece of bread.

Nutrition:
Servings: 1
Calories: 328
Calories from Fat: 85
Total Fat: 9.6g
Saturated Fat: 1.7g
Cholesterol: 49mg
Sodium: 1680mg
Carbohydrates: 36.3g
Dietary Fiber: 2.8g
Protein: 24.4g

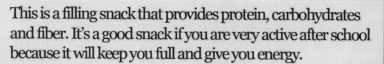

This is a filling snack that provides protein, carbohydrates and fiber. It's a good snack if you are very active after school because it will keep you full and give you energy.

Celery Canoe & Peanut Butter

TIMOTHY H. AGE 10, OHIO

THIS SNACK WILL KEEP
THE SPRING IN YOUR FEET!

SNACK-KING

Ingredients:
1 Celery Stick
1 Tbs. Peanut Butter

Instructions:
Place peanut butter in
the groove of the celery stick.

Nutrition:
Servings: 1
Calories: 114
Calories from Fat: 74
Total Fat: 8.2g
Saturated Fat: 1.6g
Cholesterol: 0mg
Sodium: 126mg
Carbohydrates: 5.4g
Dietary Fiber: 2g
Protein: 4.4g

10

This is a low-calorie snack with protein, fiber and carbohydrates. Remember, peanut butter is good for you but you
shouldn't eat too much because it's high in calories.

Edgy Veggie Pizza

THOMAS P. AGE 10, OHIO

Ingredients:

7.5 oz. of biscuits, plain or buttermilk, commercially baked
1 cup, Tomato products, canned sauce
6 oz. Cheese, Mozzarella, part skim milk
¼ cup Onions, raw, cut into smaller pieces
¼ cup Broccoli, raw, cut into smaller pieces
¼ cup Peppers, sweet green, raw, cut into small pieces

Instructions:

Separate biscuits and flatten to make crust.
Spread tomato sauce on flattened biscuit.
Add veggies (onion, broccoli and peppers).
Sprinkle with cheese.
Bake in oven using temperature indicated on biscuits.
Bake until biscuit crust is brown .

Nutrition:
Servings: 6
Calories: 222
Calories from Fat: 95
Total Fat: 10.5g
Saturated Fat: 3.8g
Cholesterol: 16mg
Sodium: 753mg
Carbohydrates: 22.1g
Dietary Fiber: 1.4g
Protein: 9.9g

This snack is a good way to get in your veggies. It has carbohydrates and protein but can be high in fat. Using low fat biscuits or whole wheat pita bread will make it a healthier snack.

Groovy Blueberry Smoothie

LASHAWN W. AGE 9, MISSOURI

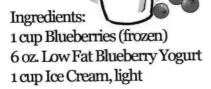

Ingredients:
1 cup Blueberries (frozen)
6 oz. Low Fat Blueberry Yogurt
1 cup Ice Cream, light

Instructions:
Place all of the ingredients into a blender.
Mix until well blended.
Pour equal amounts into two glasses and serve.

HAPPY & HEALTHY SIPPIN'!

SKIP DRIVE-THRU

Nutrition:
Servings: 2
Calories: 177
Calories from Fat: 26
Total Fat: 2.9g
Saturated Fat: 1.5g
Cholesterol: 8mg
Sodium: 74mg
Carbohydrates: 32.7g
Dietary Fiber: 2.1g
Protein: 5g

12

With carbohydrates, protein, calcium and fiber, this is a tasty low fat snack. Blueberries are high in vitamin C and help keep you healthy.

Tooty-Fruit and Marshmallows

ANGELA C. AGE 10, TEXAS

Ingredients:
¼ cup Roasted Almonds, without salt
2 cups Peaches, canned with juice
¼ cup Marshmallows
½ cup Whipped Topping

Nutrition:
Servings: 4
Calories: 119
Calories from Fat: 45
Total Fat: 5g
Saturated Fat: 0.5g
Cholesterol: 0mg
Sodium: 6mg
Carbohydrates: 16.1g
Dietary Fiber: 2.6g
Protein: 2.5g

Instructions:
Drain peaches and put into a bowl.
Mix nuts, marshmallows and
whipped topping with fruit.

THIS IS A SWEET TREAT THAT KEEPS YOU LIGHT ON YOUR FEET!

CLAIRE SPRINGS

This snack has carbohydrates, fiber and protein from the nuts. You can make it healthier by using less whipped topping and marshmallows.

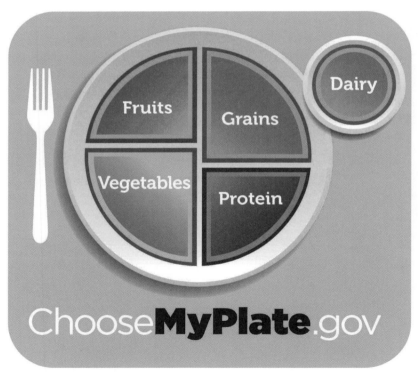

COLOR DARBY BOINGG AND THE SUPER CENTEAM 5!

ALWAYS REMEMBER TO HELP CLEAN UP
AFTER MAKING MEALS
FOR YOURSELF AND OTHERS!

16

FROM THE KITCHEN OF:
CHEF_____
NAME OF   (YOUR NAME HERE)
RECIPE:_____

INGREDIENTS:

COPY YOUR FAVORITE RECIPE
AND GIVE IT TO SOMEONE
AS A SPECIAL TREAT!

FROM THE KITCHEN OF:
CHEF_____
NAME OF   (YOUR NAME HERE)
RECIPE:_____

INGREDIENTS:

COPY YOUR FAVORITE RECIPE
AND GIVE IT TO SOMEONE
AS A SPECIAL TREAT!

FROM THE KITCHEN OF:
CHEF_____
NAME OF   (YOUR NAME HERE)
RECIPE:_____

INGREDIENTS:

COPY YOUR FAVORITE RECIPE
AND GIVE IT TO SOMEONE
AS A SPECIAL TREAT!